russ woods

Artifice Books
Chicago

ARTIFICE BOOKS

Published by Artifice Books, an imprint of Curbside Splendor Publishing, Inc., Chicago, Illinois in 2014.

First Edition
Copyright © 2014 by Russ Woods
Library of Congress Control Number: 2014931538

ISBN 978-0-9888258-0-2

Cover Design Russ Woods
Layout James Tadd Adcox

Manufactured in the United States of America.

www.artificebooks.com

contents

wolf doctors

writing prompt #1

A magic elevator that turns all occupants into sheer granite cliffs.

FOREVER PARTY

I am always having a party. When I am in the shower in the morning, shampoo party. This is how I live. Everything I do is a party. A funeral? That's just a party with a new ghost. Yesterday I was having a watching TV alone party, which, as many of you partiers know, can easily slip into a going to bed early party, a but not after setting my alarm party, because you can't forget that you have a work party early the next morning. & by work party I don't mean a collective party at my place of work because I like to think of those as work party parties. I just mean going to work, to do my job, which I interpret as a party, because that's the kind of lady I am. I'm a party gal. My work party today was great. My work party today was great until a flock of crows crashed my work party, crashed through the windows & covered every surface. The crows made me nervous, & there was all the broken glass. I asked the crows what they were doing there & they ended up coming home with me. Sometimes that kind of thing happens at a party. They came home with me & I drew a hot bath party but forgot to lock the door & they landed all over my naked, wet body. It was one of the crazier parties I've had. Three crows drowned. I wrapped their tiny bodies in soft white cloth & threw them a funeral (aka new ghost party). I thought I would never stop crying.

and I know that our parts can fit together in a certain frantic way. 700 million years ago there were no eyes. This whole light dimension of seeing and being seen of me seeing you and you seeing me was exactly null. Nature seeps new inventions. Solar flares have been known to cause heartache. Our species is founded on original doubt. This is the beginning of the poem.

I want my last meal to be a live bear. I want him to be delivered to me on a platter that is comically small, and I want to go up to him and try to take a bite and just get mauled to shit. In the best case scenario I would walk up, pretend to shake his hand, and he would lay down and I would settle in and he would let me start gnawing his leg. But just for a minute. I would even get through the fur get a solid chunk of his meat get to taste what living bear flesh tastes like before his enormous paw comes down crushing my skull. What a saint, that bear. This is the poem's middle.

This is one of those poems that you see in a literary magazine and you skip because there are too many words. Don't worry, I do it too. It's okay. I am now talking to the people who did not read this poem. People who did not read this poem: I want you to go outside the building you're currently in. I want you to smoke a cigarette. If you do not have a cigarette, I want you to go buy a pack and smoke one. I want you to then keep smoking them whenever you have free time. I want you to become addicted to cigarettes so you become a little more like me because I am addicted to cigarettes. I want you to curl your fingers around each new one like they are these tiny miracles, to feel sad about each one you throw out your car window. Not for the environment. *Not for the environment.* But for the sadness that comes with seeing that tiny miracle disappear. This addiction is something you can treasure and I feel a little less bad about encouraging you in this direction because you are the people who did not read my poem. This is almost the end of the poem.

I made a Facebook status update that said I wanted to drive my car into the south fork of the Chicago River and jump out at the last minute. Or maybe even not jump out. I was in a bad mood. They call that part of the river bubbly creek because there are rotting pieces of dead animals from the stockyards of the industrial revolution still decaying, releasing gas that makes the water bubble. Three days later I read on the news that they found a car in the south fork of the Chicago River. There was a body inside. Part of me was afraid afraid that the police would call up my wife and start calling her ma'am and tell her the body was mine.

CATS

There are three times as many cats in this room as I would like for there to be. There are eight cats in this room and I would like for there to be two and a bloody third of a cat, still a little bit alive. I think this would create some nice drama in this particular room, the cat room. This ship is a mighty vessel, one known for its many delightful rooms, and I think two cats and a bloody stump that is one third of another cat would perfectly suit our visitors experience in this room. Also it would transition nicely to the sad room next door. I am a horrible man.

WANNA BE A BALLER/SHOT CALLER

I feel like a king. I don't want to have these hiding places you don't know about. The things I read lately are making me incredible. Today I saw a baby and thought about how his face was the size of my palm. Let's walk around the swap-o-rama and learn to like instant coffee. Let's make pigeon sounds. I am thinking about how much of your hair could fit in my mouth. I now understand wanting to kill yourself in the ocean.

WHAT ARE OUR MOTIVES

We were sitting in a cafe, by the window, and you were trying to tell me something, but I was distracted, watching a road construction crew across the street. *He has been in intensive care for the past week,* you said. The men in their orange vests had taken cables from their truck. They attached it to something in a manhole. *I want to visit him soon. I think we both should go.* I stirred my coffee idly. The men began to haul an anaconda the size of a tree trunk out of the sewer. *Do you think that's a good idea,* you said. *Sure,* I said, as the men coiled up the anaconda and put it in a second truck that had arrived. *You don't think anyone will wonder what our motives are?* The men got the snake in the truck. It seemed to be dead, or possibly tranquilized. *What are our motives,* I said. The second truck sped away and a third one arrived. I sipped my coffee. You said, *well, you know I don't mean anything but the best, he and I were always so close.* The men opened the third truck and began to pull out a second snake, this one a boa, maybe half as thick, but easily twice as long, and clearly alive. The waitress came and brought you a second coffee. *But you know, there's still what happened with Carol. They'll think we're these horrible people, and I don't want anyone to think we mean anything but the best.* I took another sip. *I don't think anyone will think that. He and you were always so close. They all know that.* The men had gotten the new snake, the boa, halfway into the manhole, but seemed to be struggling as the snake tried to slither backwards through the grip of the cables and the men's hands. *I suppose you're right,* you said. *I just worry.* The crew finally got the snake in the manhole, the third truck left, and they began cleaning up the worksite. My coffee was nearly gone by this point and I noticed something in the bottom of the mug. *I know, but I think it'll be fine,* I said, as I fished the thing out with a spoon. *What in the world,* you said. I poured the contents of the spoon onto a napkin. A little gasping mouse body, brown and wet, lay there between us.

SPACE

Emma said space is where all of us are existing, always, here. None of us are not existing in space, she said. Lifestyles outside of space are impossible, but you can try. I told her thanks. I almost told her she hadn't answered my question, but I had forgotten what my question was, so maybe she had answered it. I began to think of questions that her answer may have been appropriate for. Space. Her cheeks were wet from the rain. Space. We were outdoors. Space. My hair was longer than I had remembered. Space. Everything at once was trying to get my attention. Space. We were touching now, like the skinny ends of two tree branches that couldn't find the place they both grew from.

writing prompt #2

This is a poem. This is me shooting you in the face from point blank range with a t-shirt gun. This is a poem.

i am / popping
a blimp / miles deep
in the ocean / this feeling
doesn't go away / deja vu is a seizure
symptom / but that doesn't take
the magic out / we leave presents
on doorsteps / of locks we stole
and in heavy water / warmer water
hugging isn't / even the word
for what i want / to do to you
i will break / your bones

CHAIN / SMOKE

there is a studio apt near kedzie / inside my actual / heart
like a magic school / bus and smoke is clouding / its way
out the cracked windows probably / i am a dragon or like /
you know the bible / describes three different things / we
made into just hell / / [i picked summer] / / i am splitting
atoms into smaller / atoms they don't come apart right / &
we wake up choking / under the sheets / / cigarettes are
for sharing / but i never use them that way / & how many
meals can cereal be / / [all of them] / / now is the time for
a sudden / big breath but its not coming / & i can't seem
to find anyplace to / sneeze today chad / redden told me /
there are 1000 other books / w 1000 other hells / & 1000
other times to watch when / harry met sally / / sideburns
hoodie grapes billy / crystal says he reads the last / page of
every book in / case he dies & weather patterns / are for
this & i hoped / i hoped i / hoped you'd call but / there was
nothing

CLOSE-UP PHOTO OF FLOWERS WITH LEAVES

touching your hair is a slow death /
single parent families and holding
tighter / tighter. keep your chin up
ballerina. wasting time we are wast-
ing / time. you made me coffee and I
appreciate that, glow-worm. dressed
for the weather, holding. / in my
swimsuit i will dive in the ocean / i
will swim in the waves / like a con-
gress of wolf doctors / scrubbing
themselves down.

you are a double rainbow
& i am a waterfall & i am
showing you how beautiful
you are in a million moving
fragments.

/

you are a mighty sea captain
& i am a long john silvers
waitress & you are crouching
behind the counter & i am
sneaking you hushpuppies.

/

you are a hippopotamus
with a broken leg & i am
a tiny bird & i am cleaning
your teeth & i know this
is not helping but this

/

is all i can do.
you are a sleeping frost
giant & i am a cow & you
are snoring & i am licking
your leg & this is how we
will create the world.

/

you are a beautiful dark-haired
child & i am a plague
of cholera & i am skipping
you & taking everyone else
so we can be alone together.

/

you are a winding labyrinth
& i am a plate of scrambled
eggs & i don't know if you
get hungry but hey, eggs.

/

you are a world tennis
champion & i am a world
tennis champion & i am
going to make you the best
coffee i know how.

/

you are a locomotive
& i am a salad bar
& how can we ever
finally be together.

/

i am a barber &
you are a tangle
that has confounded
my scissors & i have
nothing but admiration

& respect for you,
my greatest opponent.

/

i am a leaf & you are
the ground & i have
been waiting my whole
life to fall into you.

/

you are a beefy blonde
architect & i am an irregular
rhombus & you keep
drawing me despite my
structurally unsound
dimensions & angles.

your buildings keep collapsing.
you can no longer get work.
but here i am again.
you drew me.

the barely contained chaos
of our / curls echos the
way we feel inside / this is
a snakeskin jacket / and for
me it's a symbol of my indi-
viduality / and my belief / in
personal freedom / pimp c
is a beverage / we are drink-
ing / from speaker cones
/ and it is making us glow
/ like diamonds in light /
(up against that wood) /
(up against that wood) /
stars and parties / are better
when it's late

BLACK HART

96% of the universe is dark / matter nothing really / mat-
ters a divorce is an infinitesimal / semantic shift love / and
a heroin high / are both just pleasant / chemical experiences
the only importance / in the world that matters / is assigned
by you and it matters / only in your tiny / meaningless world
/// all human
intelligence and achievement is us / good at a game we made
/ up & we're the only / ones playing it death / is everywhere
/ always and you / smell it / so often / that your brain / can't
distinguish this is why babies / cry death is also objectively /
meaningless and all of this / is liberating / & should be & i
am / measuring my stuntedness by reactions / of people who
care about me dead / leaves aren't like dead / bodies but like
dead / skin i keep forgetting a bigger heart / is what i need
more / or less of chorus verse / chorus but sometimes the /
chorus is a single sustained / word worlds are setting around
us / and you, my lovely / my deer, my empty set / can shake
me like you never / never shake a baby

CUT STAR

the mass of love density is a cut star / flee-
ing / heart condition / heat stroke / missing
things for all time of this / personal exchange
over / the mass of love density is a cut star /
don't free me / (don't free me) / astral pro-
jection in the hands of a saint / solar giants
manipulating the body / from a great remove
/ moving arms legs head / clumsy like clay
breaking / being gently rolled / between
enormous fingertips

writing prompt #3

A teen romance about a love triangle between Lake Superior and two of Jupiter's moons. Feel free to pick any two moons you like! My favorite are Callisto and Ganymede.

CITY-GIRL

I used to be a city but now I'm a girl. It took a long time for me to change from a city to a girl and the in-between stages were kind of stupid but it feels good having arms and feet instead of buildings and stoplights. It feels good being my own comptroller and my own slumlord.

It feels good being a girl and if you look close you can tell I was a city before. Inside me there are city things going on. Inside me it's still loud.

Inside me there is a woman who loves her dog so much that she filmed it sleeping and projected it thirty feet high onto the side of her apartment building. A dog-eye twitches and a whole window seems to move. The building is dog-breathing.

Last week there was a nightmare and the whole sidewalk broke in half the long way in front of the building. Birds took turns landing on the break looking for bugs and they found a few. Pedestrians were having trouble and so the woman came out and helped them push their babies and she could feel the babies pushing back.

NO SKIN

Christopher was born without skin. He slid from his mother all organs barely held in with muscle and sinew. Naked at 35 he is still covered in a wide net of scars from the unconventional patchwork grafting the doctors did. Like a skin quilt they sewed onto him. Like Edward Scissorhands. Like Herman Munster. Christopher loves it. It makes him feel like a superhero who could at any minute discover his powers. He has seriously considered getting tattoos at all the scars' intersections. Little points of black ink all over his body emphasizing the thin white lines. Maybe cryptic symbols. Something badass. Maybe he should shave his head.

FACTORY

Christopher worked at a factory where meat was condensed into little tins. He got up at six am every day and drove thirty-five minutes to put ham in cans. At home he grew apples and ate spaghetti. He liked action movies and went on dates from the Internet. He put the thing in the cans with the machines all day. Sometimes the machines hummed things at him. One time they said life is a cloud of loneliness but we can get through it.

FISH

Christopher liked the way fish felt in his hands. Slimy and then occasional the catch of a scale here and there. Catfish were his favorite, though. Sometimes he looked on job websites for work in fish hatcheries. His ideal job, he thought, would be getting paid to touch catfish and smoke cigarettes all day long.

HIGHWAY

Christopher loved driving down the highway. He loved how the signs had names for towns nowhere near him tempting him to drive to Memphis instead of work or Detroit instead of the grocery store. The other fantasy the highway gave him was that of destruction and death, of his and everyone else's cars turning over at full speed, their hoods peeling back like sardine tins and his and everyone else's skulls grinding huge smears of blood and flesh across the pavement. This was fantastic.

STREAM

Christopher wanted to live in a mountain stream in the winter. He wanted to push his fingers into the mud and watch the salmon spawning. He currently lived above a taqueria on Halsted. Sometimes at night he would open his bathroom window and stand in the shower with the nozzle on all the way cold and feel the wind and the water trickling down over him and look out at the people milling up and down the street and pretend. He was a bear. He was going to eat them.

writing prompt #4

Write a crime drama using all of the following words:

dogs dogs dogs dogs dogs dogs dogs dogs dogs dogs dogs dogs dogs dogs dogs dogs dogs dogs dogs dogs dogs dogs dogs dogs dogs dogs dogs dogs dogs d

DOG-ARMS

I want to have dogs for arms. Dog-arms. I want to open my dual dog-mouths like fists and watch them eat Science Diet. I want to shake your hand with them and tell you good job so your palm can guess what the teeth could do. I want to make them wear outfits and take classes and like children. When I hug you with my dog-arms you will feel warm and embraced and fulfilled and afraid more completely than a hug has ever made you feel before. When I make sandwiches their floppy tongues will leave spittle dots on my paper plate. People will love me for my dog-arms and I will love my dog-arms and I will be kind to them but tell them no when I have to. Kind, yet firm. They will eventually eat me and this is how I will die. In a whirlwind of teeth and bones, blood and fur, armed and armless. I love you, I love you, goodnight.

HORSEBEAUTIFUL

I'm going to start a magazine called HorseBeautiful about how I miss you already. We'll only publish large photos of beautiful horses with broken hearts. There will be no front or back cover. There will be no staples and it will just keep falling apart like we did. HorseBeautiful will have 10000 subscribers and they will all live inside the ocean. All of the boxes with the issues will just be thrown into the ocean. Environmental activists won't care because they all miss you too. It will go on for 100 issues and then the government will create a law to stop its publication because it was too sad. The back issues will be added to the curriculum in important universities all over the country. They will be considered influential texts in the exciting new field of Crying. Hugs will be declared the new universal currency, and their value will be determined not by quantity but by effectiveness. You will be the richest person alive.

A LOVE POEM

There are two men in an Aspen grove in Colorado and they are touching their foreheads together. Their foreheads are sweaty and their sweat mingles and drips down into the dirt and makes sweat-mud, which is saltier than regular mud. The men's foreheads and the men are in the grove and the grove is shaped like a forehead. The grove is next to a freshwater lake which is also shaped like a forehead and there is a town on the lake shore which is inhabited by forehead-people. There is a mountain there called mount forehead and deer and bears and raccoons live on it. Somewhere there is a small country whose national bird is the forehead and the men, right now, are only speaking the native language of this country, and they are doing the national dance of this country, though they don't know it. I am watching these men from a forehead-shaped hot air balloon hovering over the aspen grove and you are with me and I want to kiss you on your you-know-what.

We're in Russia. I pulled the car off of the side of the road, into the snow. The snow was everywhere, as far as I could see. *We're in Russia!* I yelled out. I lifted my arms up and started spinning. *WE. ARE. IN. RUSSIA.* I kneeled down beside my car and scooped some of the snow into my hands. *We're in Russia.* I whispered to it. I shifted the handful into just my left hand, trying to spill as little as possible. I gently stroked the top of the handful with my fingertips. *Russiiiaaaaaa...*

I AM WATCHING A BOXING MATCH

I am watching a boxing match between two fighters without gloves. They are both crying. Their fighting names are me and you and these names are emblazoned on the backs of their elaborate shimmering capes that they shed before approaching the center of the ring, before the first bell, and they begin the fight passive aggressively, giving each other worrisome looks and saying things like I'm just trying to look out for you before eventually ramping things up and reminding the other of the times they were unthoughtful. The referee is allowing it this time and all this is taking place in a tiny stadium smaller than your fingernail and I never find out who wins because they take so long that I get too old and need glasses and they're too small and I don't know what's going on anymore. My memory is shot and it's hard to keep track of anything and these two fighters they keep going or at least I assume they do and the referee dies. I know that much. I know the referee dies because I saw that and attended his tiny funeral and got to see the microscopic tears on the faces of his tiny wife and her tiny, tiny children.

YOU ARE ACTUALLY A BABY DEER AND I'M NOT GOING TO LET THAT GET IN THE WAY OF OUR POTENTIAL FUTURE RELATIONSHIP

There is seriously an island in the south pacific that is entirely covered in fragments of human teeth and all of these teeth are from people whose parents took them from underneath their children's pillows. Spoiler alert the tooth fairy is parents. Anyway the teeth are in fragments because I have walked over every inch of this island looking for a secret code that was placed there by the Incas that was placed there by Tibetan monks that was placed there by George Clooney's hidden twin that was placed there by an animate meteor with a bad childhood who now places secret codes on tooth-islands. This secret code will let me into a room in a broom closet at the pentagon and I know after I duck all the security lasers and put lead sand in my pockets until I weigh exactly 203.4 pounds and use my hidden Clooney twin retinal replicating glasses I can gain access to this pentagon-room where they are doing top secret research on the unpredictable physiological effects of your hair-smell. I read about this on WikiLeaks and I need to get in this room because you left your phone at my apartment i want to make sure you have your phone.

writing prompt #5

Write a poem on the topography of your internal organs. Eat the poem. Mail a short length of your small intestine to a literary journal. Next, try sending it with computers!

i want to jump from space with you sponsored by redbull we will ride in a hot air balloon and we will be in one space suit that is specially modified for two people and so we will be kissing the whole time in the balloon and then when they go down the checklist to make sure we don't die we will keep having to stop kissing to make sure we are doing the right things and the mission control guy will have to keep telling us guys guys jesus guys this is important and we will say yes yes this is important but we will keep going back to kissing and eventually once we get through the whole checklist we will step out onto the skateboard-sized-platform so so high up in the air and we will jump into space sponsored by redbull which they say gives you wings but you already had wings and so we'll fly around for awhile because i secretly made a place in the back of our suit where your wings could come out and we will fly and kiss and fly and kiss and spin through the clouds and the announcer on the webcast will say oh no they are in a spiral but we are just spinning and kissing and i will drink part of a redbull and put it in your mouth with my mouth and you will drink part of a redbull and put it in my mouth with your mouth and we will spiral down down down through the stratosphere and the clouds and we won't even use the parachute because your wings will land us beautifully in new mexico where everyone will be waiting for us and cheering guys you broke so so many records also we didn't know you had wings and you'll say yeah that's a secret i've been keeping and i'll be so proud of you because i love your wings and now the world loves you for your wings but i don't love you for your wings i love you for how you remind me that we are tiny and meaningless and sponsored by redbull and that life is tiny and short and not sponsored by shit and we can do whatever we goddamn want we can jump from space and kiss and fuck and hug an endangered species and get put in jail in south america and break out of jail with the key i swallowed before we hugged that endangered species holy shit good thing i swallowed that key right?

YOU HAVE PERFECT HAIR I AM A TIGER

you have perfect
hair! i am a tiger that
will sneak into your
room at night & whisper
about how we are
always standing
under waterfalls,
especially
when we are
just together
breathing there
in bed.

I'M REALLY BIG I'M YOUR MOM

I'm really
big I'm your
mom listen to
me listen
I'm only
trying to
help
honey
big listen
to me swe-
etie listen

listen
list-
en.

YOU ARE SO BEAUTIFUL I'M CALLING THE COPS.

I want to
go to bed

in your
hair. This

is an
emerg-

ency.
100000

children
are scream-

ing fire fire
this guy's

heart is on
fire call

911 before
we all burn

right up!
dear children:

it's too
late. you're

toast.
goners.

love,
russ

MOON STONE

It is afternoon & we
are taking turns trying to

open a bottle of cherry
coke & you laugh

when I use my teeth
and then my teeth hurt.

It is morning & we are
in my car & I am driving

you to class & you touch
my knee when we are

singing along to joni
mitchell.

It is late at night & you lean
over me to make sure your alarm is set.

It is early morning & we are
sleeping longer today & I

roll on the other side away
from you & don't want to

but my arm is asleep from
lying on the other side.

I am driving home from seeing
you & there is a crowd of people

singing some days they
last longer than others

but this day by the lake
went too fast.

It is a city-morning & I am
walking in it & playing easy

scrabble with it & you are not
there but you are totally there

and I say hello
hello hello.

ROTTING APPLE SUTRA

every time you inhale
you are creating an entire universe
that has never existed before.
every time you exhale
you are destroying that universe.

my fist is about the size of a
bird body and there are wings
i'm willing to give it.
i want to push my lungs
against a concrete wall
and feel my breath
getting rougher.
look at my gums! pieces of
my tongue fall out when i drink.
i am not a healthy person.

but you can pinch the whole world
at once in half--in half!--
with your eyelids or maybe
more like squish it to soft black
like an old apple you can
sink your heel through.

we are all grinding our teeth.
we are all selling off our fingers
and we are not asking very much
for them. please buy our fingers.
we are an event that exponentially amplifies
all emotion passing through us.
we are the fucking christmas of reality.

i read about how a man in sri lanka
tried to beat some world record
for being buried alive.
he didn't beat the world record
because he died down there.
when they dug him up he had stopped
breathing. i'm not sure if that's
called exhumation or not.

this poem was written to be screamed.
this poem was written to be written
microscopically on a grain of rice.
i am not yelling words they're sound
and everything is crashing.
sound doesn't collide with ears
sound shakes the mother
fucking molecular foundation
of us and everything.

TAQUERIA SAN JOSE

We know the sun is pear-shaped.
I have brought you this pear to illustrate my point.

Everyone in this restaurant won't listen to me.
I hold my pear up, hold it up to show you.

You aren't interested, even though I tell you about
how they published my work in Canada.

I feel like I have twelve arms and they each are sore.
My physics is immaculate but

that doesn't matter here it's just tacos tacos.
Just these sweaty children crying dude

shut up about the sun.

writing prompt #6

Write a poem on paper made of someone else's hair. Become a noble-man. Get real good at hopscotch.

DOGS

I.

There are 800 dogs in this room. This is a large room. This is a noisy room. All of the dogs are awake. All of the dogs are moving. Some of the dogs are playing. Some are using their noses to push things. Some of the dogs are not getting along very well. 800 dogs is a large number of dogs. I am walking though the room and I am petting each fourth dog. The ceiling of the room is painted with clouds on a light blue background. I look at the ceiling while I pet a dog. The dog is a mean dog, and he bites my hand. My hand is bleeding. The painted cloud above me is shaped vaguely like a dog. I pick up a small dog and try to move away from the one that bit me.

II.

Erin drew a bath to bathe her dog. Erin's bathtub was a claw-foot one, and she liked to imagine it walking around on the feet. Erin's feet were person-feet, not claw-feet. Erin's dog's feet were claw-feet. Not like the tub's claw-feet, just like regular dog claw-feet. Sara held her dog with one hand as the tub filled with water. Erin's dog stood nobly in the rising water while she scooped handfuls of water onto his back. The sun came in through the window. The water went *shhhhhhhhh*. The mirror reflected the top of Erin's ginger head, slightly bobbing as she shook the bottle of dog-shampoo.

III.

This is a dog poem. There are meanings in this poem that are too high pitched for humans to hear. I don't even know what they are. I am a human. This poem is not for us. This is a dog poem.

IV.

I am a dog and you are a dog and we are dogs in love. I lick your snout. You lick my snout. These are dog-kisses. We are walking down the sidewalk together. We don't have leashes. We don't need leashes. I am walking you and you are walking me. You are scratching your back on a tree in the park. I am scratching my back on a tree in the park. I wish we could hold hands and walk at the same time. We run down a hill and its fun. We climb up the hill and it's less fun, but still fun because you're here. We try to see whose tongue is longer. It's hard to tell, we both have pretty long tongues. When we hug we have to lie down. This is not a problem. The sky is blue up above us and we lie down in leaves and hug. We lick snouts again. Nothing is impossible. We are dogs.

MANY HOOVES

We want you to know that we love you. We treasure the golden locks of your hair, and want to kiss your sweet lips. The way you look down and smile, unsure how to deal with the smallest compliment makes our hearts lift up in our throats. We are sorry we are a large herd of angry bulls, charging toward you, about to kill you. We cannot control our instincts, cannot counter the inertia of our rampage. We cannot act or think as a group except to feel, together, wildly and passionately a longing, desire and sorrow so intense regarding you. You have set us ablaze with your gentleness and intelligence.

You can never know how each of us scream with desperation to our legs, to our muscles to STOP. To at least divert ourselves in any direction other than the one that will surely lead to your destruction. To redirect our energy, to sacrifice ourselves, even, if it were to come to it. It is with bleak, bottomless despair that we resign ourselves to this: the destruction of the only thing we have ever loved. We are a large herd of angry bulls and we are deeply, deeply sorry. Our lives from this moment on shall be meaningless. Some of us will move on to live out our days in a haze of regret and darkest depression, while others will find ways to off ourselves, throw our bodies from cliffs or in front of oncoming vehicles massive enough to cause our end. But for now we are united in this singular emotion: we are wholly devoted to you, in love.

This whole town smells like beef. It smells like a thousand cows accidentally stepped into a thousand barbecue pits at once and it started raining sauce. The mayor has left because he is too hungry. He left a note and the note says coleslaw.

BIRTHDAYS

I am wearing a special outfit for you today, on this day, your birthday. Your birthday is my national holiday. The only one I celebrate. This shirt is made of gold thread, yes thread made from actual gold. Look at how shiny i am for you for your birthday! And my shoes!

These shoes are diamond shoes, made from diamonds! Diamond shoes, just for yous. And my pants, they're made of your favorite song. Yes, they are made entirely of "Wonderful Tonight" by Eric Clapton. You didn't know I knew, did you? Put your ear on my pants. No, don't be afraid, it's your birthday! This pants-song is for you! Listen. Shhhh. Darlin' you look wonderful tonight. Yep. These pants. They're the coup-de-gras of my your-birthday outfit. The coop dee grass for you. The hat? Sure that IS made of cheese pierogies, your favorite food. But that's nothing compare to the song-pants. What I really wanted to show you was the pants. It looks like visiting hours are over now, though, so I'm going to have to say goodbye. I love you. Happy birthday!

LAKE BEACH

I was a dog-trainer riding a bicycle on the north avenue lake beach. It had been raining & the sand was wet & my tires sank into it. I rode my bike into the edge of water to get my tires wet but I was moving so slowly that I almost fell over. The clouds parted & the sun came out & it began to get really hot so I took off my shirt & used it to tie my bike tires together. I threw my bike into the lake. I thought about all the dogs I had trained. There was a Dalmatian I missed. I thought about the Dalmatian & began crying & waded into the water to get my bike. My shirt had come untied from it. My shirt was gone. I dug a hole in the sand & planted my bike in it & watered it with lake water. I lay there for months & watched it grow a bright blue, icy-looking plant that stood out & looked strange against the skyline of the city. I picked a fruit from the plant & the plant bled on the sand where the fruit came from. I got scared & put the fruit in my pocket & dug my bike back up but it was a horrible dog-creature now. Its fur was encrusted with sand. I tried to train it. Heel I called out. Heel. The dog-creature ripped my arm from my shoulder. It hurt tremendously & I began screaming & crying. The wound had no blood in it. I felt like I needed to bleed but I couldn't. I tried bleeding for a long evening while the dog-creature watched docudramas on netflix. You are a good dog, I told him, but you are not my dog. I went back home. Later that week I reported my bike stolen & put up flyers. I got one call about it but it was the dog-creature, just bleeding into the phone, mocking me. What are you doing, I said. What are you even doing.

SPIDERS

When I was eight years old I used to leave peanut butter for the spiders in our basement. There was an empty closet under the stairs where the ceiling was shaped like the underside of stairs and there were webs down there. I didn't always see the spiders alive, or at least sometimes I couldn't tell if they were alive. I liked spending time with them when I felt creepy. I don't know if they liked peanut butter. I didn't really know what else to give them. I would just leave the jar open down there and then throw it away and put a new jar out whenever it got hard inside. I used to try to make them crawl on me. On my legs. In my hair. Somebody told me spider bites could kill you if they were the right kind of spider like a black widow spider or a brown recluse spider. I'm pretty sure our spiders weren't like that but I wasn't too worried about it. I was eight. The spiders seemed nice. My mom thought I ate a lot of peanut butter.

writing prompt #7

Try walking with your arms below the ground for a few minutes. How does it make you feel?

WITHIN THE FIRST TWO MONTHS OF ITS OPERATION, THE FACILITY HAD SEVENTEEN CASES OF SEVERE LEAD POISONING LEADING TO HALLUCINATIONS & INSANITY, & THEN FIVE DEATHS IN QUICK SUCCESSION.

Within the first two months of its operation, the facility had three employees gain cat parts. These employees actually grew tails, extra ears, paws, etc. To be specific, two tails, three ears & one paw were grown. Most of these were on one specific employee. He is less cute than one might think.

Within the first two months of its operation, the facility had a brief plague of dance fever. Work was stalled for five hours while the entire staff could not help but get down with their bad selves. No injuries were sustained during this time.

Within the first two months of its operation, the facility had sixteen fatalities. These were Mortal Kombat-style fatalities, replete with a disembodied voice booming "FINISH HIM". One babality was also recorded, & the victim has since been adopted by a very happy young couple in Hoboken who had been trying to have their own for some time now.

Within the first two months of its operation, the facility had exactly one appearance of a delightful rainbow horse who gave everyone candy. This was really, really fun.

Within the first two months, the facility had an all-staff game of Operation. The board took up a whole floor of the facility & the tweezers had to be operated by forklift. The buzzer was hooked up to the intercom system & Head of Human Resources Elaine Thompson dominated the proceedings with a phenomenal record of 14-1. The one game Elaine lost was to her boss & many suspect the match may have been thrown because she wanted to still have a job afterward.

Within the first two months of its operation, the facility went through a really bad breakup & spent most of its time in its dorm room writing a concept album about cats. It went vegan & drank soymilk out of those little boxes you put a straw in like for juice. The facility wasn't a very good vegan & mostly ate Nutter Butters.

Within the first two months of its operation, the facility asked for a Furby for Christmas but instead received a new Furby, terrifying nightmare edition. The facility kept the creature on its desk but would awake in the morning to find it posed as if caught in the act of strangling & or/torturing other toys in the facility's room. One morning the Furby was found waterboarding mister potato head with juicy juice & ever since then Furby has been relocated to his new home at the bottom of the toy chest.

Within the first two months of its operation the facility created a strictly enforced policy that all interoffice memos be drafted only in medieval blackletter script, & that the contents should be fraught with arcane gnostic subtext. This lasted until Judi in administration showed a marked gift for prophesy & predicted the facility's downfall as well as a series of dire misfortunes that would plague Carl, the office manager, to his last days.

Within the first two months of its operation the facility experienced an unpredictable amount of graffiti that seemed to appear with alarming regularity on walls & equipment throughout the facility. Simple tags & 'throw-ups' were discovered during the first few days, & within the first two weeks larger, more elaborate pieces were discovered, including one of a majestic dragon with the face of Christopher Walken fiercely guarding a massive hoard of gold & jewels against a brave knight. Administration issued an official statement via company-wide email, saying We just don't know what to do about it. We will now think twice before specifying that we are looking for 'creative, self-motivated individuals' during the hiring process.

Within the first two months of its operation, the facility's employees began questioning their own sanity. Liliputian, humanoid figures were spotted by a large number of workers, scurrying in corners, crouched inside little-used file folders, & chewing on cat5 cable. The employees did not tell each other about these miniature office residents, but instead began resigning one-by-one when the visions persisted. The tiny people began to get more bold & would be seen executing perfect back-handsprings across the middle of the hallway & popping out of the toilet when a worker went to raise the seat. Each employee filed their resignation over the two-month span until the little ones were all that was left to keep the facility afloat. They were quite effective at this & corporate did not question how a branch operating with no employees maintained such a consistently high level of productivity. In their eyes they had received a bountiful blessing from the omnipotent gods of industry, whom they thanked monthly with burnt offerings of lamb & cattle.

writing prompt #8

The smell of the ocean as an infectious disease. Me giving it to you. You giving it to me. Us kissing a lot.

You don't even know what I look like, do you?

My name is Nathan.

GOLD PAINT

In honor of mothers day I want to share with you a fresh new beauty secret diet tip. In honor of mothers day I want to share with you a fresh new beauty secret diet tip that will make you loose thousands of weight just by breathing. Just by breathing. Are you breathing now? Yes. Before I came up here I checked. You probably didn't notice. I am so so very sneaky. In honor of mothers day I am being sneaky. Oprah Winfrey knows about this beauty secret diet tip but has been hoarding it for herself. Oprah Winfrey was determined to bring this beauty secret diet tip to her fucking grave. Oprah Winfrey has been trying to fuck us all over for years. Editors at O Magazine have lost their jobs. Editors at O Magazine have lost their families. Editors at O Magazine have begged to lose their lives but have not been allowed to, because it is a worse fate to grow old knowing you are on Oprah's bad side. In honor of mothers day I will probably be tortured for telling you about this.

I have been gargling gold paint every day since I was six years old. Notice how my skin is glowing. Notice how obese I am not. Editors at O Magazine have tried to get this out. Editors at O Magazine know what I am talking about. I have been gargling gold paint every day since I was three years old. My mother knew about this, as it is an old Appalachian tradition from centuries ago. My mother knew about this because she is a Tibetan monk. My mother knew about this because she saw it written on the back of the declaration of independence. I have been gargling gold paint every day since I was a fucking zygote. I am so tan I can lay undetected by predators in the Serengeti. I am so toned I can choke a pony. In honor of mother's day I would like to choke a pony onstage. This fresh new beauty secret diet tip will give you a stiffy. This fresh new beauty secret diet tip will henceforth be referred to as TFNBSDT. This is because the CIA. This is because the FBI. This is because the KGB. This is because the VCR. THEY ARE TAPING.

Soon the government will know how tan my skin is. Soon the government will know how fresh my locks are. Soon the government will know how slim and toned my body is. Soon the government will know how sad my feelings are. Soon the government will know about the pony. That pony was a government pony. The reason my feelings are sad is because that pony had no say in the matter. That pony was a pawn in a game he could never comprehend. That poor pony. It never asked to be a government pony. That pony wanted to grow up to be a folk singer. That pony listened to Arlo Guthrie records all day as a child, dreaming of one day growing up to be a folk singer. I have single-handedly crushed that pony's dreams. This is what this fresh new beauty secret diet tip has done to me. I have gargled gold paint every day since I was a spermatozoa and I have crushed the dreams of an innocent pony. In honor of mothers day, this is what the government is doing to us. In honor of mother's day, I would like to propose a coup. Seven hundred million years ago the world was a better place. Seven hundred million years ago the rocks were going around so toned and tanned. Seven hundred million years ago we were stuck in a time loop. Seven hundred million years ago the earth was getting all mixed up. Seven hundred million years ago TFNBSDT was never even invented. Seven hundred million years ago a plant made a decision that set us on this path. In honor of mother's day, I would like to say *fuck that plant*. My skin is so toned and my muscles are so tanned and I was sent here to give you all a message. I am a sexy, sexy voice crying out in the wilderness. I am John the Baptist as played by Dwayne "The Rock" Johnson. In honor of mother's day I have filled eighty-seven water balloons with horse urine and hung them from the rafters. The JFK assassination was a dry run. In honor of mothers day eighty-seven horsepissballoons could drop at any goddamn minute don't even fucking try me.

The editors at O magazine have sent me a message to give you all. The editors of O magazine sent secret operatives into my house to tattoo manifestos on my gums. The editors at O magazine want you to know that if they win this election we can all be saved. The editors of O magazine want you to know that if they win this election you won't have to worry about the balloons. I have been gargling gold paint every day since I was my grandfather and I want you to know that we shall overcome. In honor of mother's day the revolution will not be covered in horse piss. In honor of mother's day the revolution is just around the corner. In honor of mother's day, I would like to invite you all to look under your seats, where you will find the keys to a new version of yourself that your mother will like better. In honor of mother's day, I'm sorry for all of this, please forget this ever happened.

I PUT MY FINGERS IN YOUR EYES

because they were making too much light
i have all these feelings
we shopped in the mall until it closed
and bought so many pretzels
so many pretzels

NO FIRE

each time i
inhale there

is a catch
of breath

in me like a
slight fishhook

and the light is
too strong

selling things off
is a productive

destruction and
you come

over every single
time i call you

but there is no
staying in here

there is no
fire here in

sampled
packets

grow me tall
find my true

arm and leg
lengths for me

crush my toes
grow me all

the best deer
resistant flowers

BOATS

when i was touching
your hair and you
were touching mine

we carried
our shoes we
were alone

boats flickered
at us it
was night

they flickered
yes the beach
was beautiful i
almost cried

nothing was
coming to kill
us then

/

nothing was
coming to
save us

you weren't
there i don't
know who
you are

WHAT CATS LOOK LIKE

i am an image
on the retina
of a sparrow

of what cats
look like
when they

pounce.
you are the
instinct

in the cat's
brain stem
to catch, to

eat stuff.
we are
in love. we

are
in
love.

I FOUND YOU YOU WERE A RIVER

I found you.
You were a river
of hard apples
that I cannon-
balled into.

You were a solid
stream of make-
believe tv shows
that I had set
my alarm for.

You were a dark
room that I didn't
need to turn the
lights on in like

finding the way
to the bathroom
at night as a child.

& it was like
finding a lake
under your bed.

It was like joining
a cult & discover-
ing they all believed
in you.

It was like hiding a
a trampoline in
your closet.

It was like singing
beautiful carols
in autotune.

It was like planting
pink erasers &
then watching
them sprout.

It was like
pushing soft
erasers into
potting soil

for a joke,
maybe

but then
bam

sprouts.
& then as
if that weren't
enough:

little berries.
perfect.

THE OPPOSITE OF KILLING 1000 PEOPLE

i am going to sneak into 1000 homes
& leave 1000 bath & body works gift baskets.

replace the tile in 1000 bathrooms
while the owners are on 1000 vacations.

i will slip 1000 winning lotto
tickets under 1000 doors

& sneak all daily essential vitamins &
minerals into 1000 blueberry oatmeals.

watch me do 40000 covert chores
& send 20000 anonymous, gushing

letters to 1000 people's bosses.
they won't know what hit them.

then i will expand my purview:
all of america you are next!

i will pay your netflix bills &
cat-sit when you didn't ask me to!

you will wake up to a gleaming,
freshly waxed car & the realization

that your folgers can has been filled with real
columbian-grown, hand-roasted beans!

then much, much later, while you sleep,
maybe in late autumn when there

is no sound but the rustling
of the trees' last golden leaves,

i will come whisper in your ear,
you are as good as the opposite of dead.

writing prompt #9

Eat salt until you can feel dryness inside you. That's called fiction.

NO DEER

I was trying to keep the deer out of my horse garden. They kept getting in and eating the horses. The horses wouldn't even get that big, just foals before deer would come in and nibble their manes. Then my wife said I should just keep at it, that that was the price of growing things organically. I told her she doesn't understand and then I realized that she was a hotel, that I'd been married to a hotel this whole damn time and I formed a plan. Late at night, when she was asleep, I took a pouch of horse seeds and a few bags of mulch and snuck into her front door. She has a giant picture window that faces out of living room in her honeymoon suite, so right there I made a little bed. I threw her curtains wide open and dumped soil down on her carpet and began to plant. I've been doing this every night for weeks now, coming in and tending the horses I am growing inside my wife. I don't think she's figured it out yet, but the horses have been coming along nicely.

I EVEN ATE SOME OF THE FLOWERS AND THEY WERE GREAT

There is a giant tree in a forest in nova scotia with 1000 birds-nests and 4000 baby birds. There is a giant squid in the mariana trench that has made 3000 giant squid eggs. There is a nebula in andromeda where 10000 stars have been born. There is a follicle just above the ear of Associate US Supreme Court Justice Antonin Scalia where 5000 inches of hair have been grown. When I am kissing you I am getting 5000 inches of Justice hair in my mouth. When I am kissing you I am burning my mouth on 10000 baby stars. When I am kissing you I am squishing 3000 squishy squid eggs that feel kind of like tapioca jelly or something. When I am kissing you I am having my lips bitten by 4000 baby bird beaks. When I am kissing you I am kissing a whole universe that is super into it and is kissing me back and that universe loves me so much and that universe is this universe and that universe is you and that universe has 9E15 eyes and those eyes are looking in my eyes and now i am kissing their eyelids and some of them are weird bug eyelids and i don't even care because this feeling this feeling this feeling this feeling.

TUSCARORA WAR

I have been the Tuscarora War for years now. Ever since my cousin's wedding. I got drunk & danced like a bedsheet caught in a stiff wind. It was wonderful. Everyone was drunk except the children. The children all fell asleep on the pile of coats by the door. A pile of children on a pile of coats. Nobody could leave until the children woke up, because nobody wanted to leave their coat, which was good, because we were all too drunk to drive. I woke up later that night & I was a child who had fused with five coats. I could lift all my sleeves up & move them around like ten extra arms. I fell asleep again & woke up early in the morning as the Tuscarora War. I stretched my troops & scratched my battles & looked in the mirror. I thought I could go to sleep & wake up as the coats-child again. I went back to bed & woke up but I was still that war. I called my sister & she asked if I wanted to come with her to church. I said okay. The church was small & quiet & I felt like everyone was looking at me. I don't think they were expecting a war in their church. The preacher took me aside & gave me starlight mints. I thanked him & kissed his cheek, & one of my fires caught on his coat. He threw his coat away & said it was no problem. The coat burned into the shape of a child. I took the coat-child home & made it clothes out of more coats. You are my child, I told it. You are my child.

ILLINOIS

Illinois was the best horse I ever had. I use to ride him for hours through the trails in the woods behind our ranch. His silken fur and amber eyes were the keys to my heart. My heart was a Toyota Carolla. It was a pain in the ass to start, though, given the fact that the keys were the silken fur and amber eyes of a horse named Illinois. The horse, though! Oh the horse! I loved that horse so dearly until I had to put him down when his governor tried to sell the president's senate seat.

A JOKE

Once there was a seahorse. The seahorse lived in an apartment off of Halsted on the south side. He had a cat and a dog he really liked. One day a man knocked on his door and delivered a package. Oh gee, said the seahorse, I wonder what it is. The seahorse opened the package and inside was a note that said how are you breathing air

TWO STORIES ABOUT THE SAME THING

1. I found a book in the library that was about the stars. It had a recipe inside for making your own stars at home. It came with drugs you had to take before making the stars, to make sure they turned out right. The drugs came in a little envelope in the back that was printed with the words *shh don't tell the police.*

2. When I met you, you were wearing a blue shirt I assumed you'd borrowed from someone else. You wore it casually, like you were comfortable wearing someone else's clothes and liked they way they hung on you like an accident. You were making copies and your hair hung down over the copy machine. I came up and said hello and you showed me the thing you were making copies of. It was part of your hair that you'd cut off and only then did I notice the place you cut it off from. I asked if I could have one of the copies and you told me a story about your grandfather. You said your grandfather was a farmer. You told me he grew all the right ingredients to make bombs, and he sold them to the military. Or at least he did until they began to pressure him into sell what he grew for cheaper and cheaper. He knew he couldn't make a living on the amount they were offering and would arrest him if he began selling to someone else. *What did he do,* I asked. *He fell in love,* you said.

THE PLAY WHERE I WAS A VERY OLD HOUSE YOU LIVED IN

When we left the opening of the play we saw where I was an old house you lived in, we both agreed it wasn't very good. You looked beautiful, in your linen dress, and my hair was perfect, and fit the style of the light jacket I was wearing. You were cold, and so I handed you my light jacket, which you put on and you looked even better in it than I did. I almost said to you, *look how beautiful we both look*, but then decided that if we were to really be beautiful, we wouldn't have to say it, so I didn't. Instead I kissed your temple and we got on the train, where everyone admired us so. One of them said, *that play, wasn't that about you? You, the gentleman, you were the house, weren't you? And you, the beautiful lady, you were the wistful occupant of the house, the one who mowed the lawn with a lawnmower that turned everything to gold. And you, the gentleman, you cried soft house-tears when you saw what this beautiful woman was turning your lawn into. You couldn't handle such tenderness. Yes,* we told the man, *that was us, we were the ones in that play.* But we didn't tell him about our feelings about the play. How they left out the part where I was haunted and my ghosts scared you out. Or the part where we had a child whose wooden lungs collapsed with his first breath of air. He seemed to like the play, the play we did not think lived up to the reviews and had poor costume design. We rode home beautifully, in silence, and I thought about how gracious we had been in that particular interaction. How noble.

MURDER THE SUN

You have been living in a horrible, angry, smelly place for the past 90 days. You are irritable because you are itchy and you are itchy because of fleas. Fleas and impatience. You are impatient because you have a quest. It is your quest to murder the sun. Don't forget to murder the sun. There are lots of reasons you might forget your quest. One of them is the fleas. Don't let these be excuses. Don't blame it on the fleas. There is a sun out there and it needs to be murdered. By you. Preferably. I know you have been in a horrible, angry, smelly place for the past 90 days and I sympathize with you. Or I empathize with you. One of those. But it is very important very very important that you do not forget your quest. Your quest to M the S. D.F.T.M.T.S. Here, I'll write it on your hand.

acknowledgments

Earlier versions of portions of this manuscript have previously appeared in the following publications: *Another Chicago Magazine, Apt, Artifice Magazine, Atlas Review, The Bakery, Cityscapes 2, Dinosaur Bees, Dogzplot, Everyday Genius, For Every Year, French Press Mag, Have U Seen My Whale, ILK Journal, >kill author, Menacing Hedge, N/A, NAP, [PANK], Pear Noir!, PressBoardPress, Reality Hands, Red Lightbulbs, SP CE Lovebook 2, Spork, Untoward Magazine, Unsure If I Will Allow My Beard to Grow for Much Longer, Used Furniture Review, Whiskey Island Review,* and *Whole Beast Rag.*

The author wishes to express his thanks to Jeannette Gomes, James Tadd Adcox, Matt Rowan, Jess Dutschmann, Chadwick Redden, Sasha Fletcher, Mason Johnson, Peter Jurmu, Carrie Lorig, Brett Erik Gallagher, Brett Elizabeth Jenkins, Nathan Carter, Russell Jaffe, M Kitchell, Christopher Kelly, Susan & Larry Woods, Leif Haven, Jared Harvey, Meghan Lamb, Donald Dunbar, Mathias Svalina, Zachary Schomburg, Amber Sparks, Adam Robinson, Lindsay Hunter, Mark Cugini, Beach Sloth, Jacob Knabb, Nick Sturm, and Jordaan Mason.

about the author

Russ Woods is a poet and librarian living in Chicago. He is the currently author of three books, of which this is the first, and nine chapbooks. His poetry and collaborations have appeared widely, in magazines such as *Gulf Coast, Denver Quarterly, Guernica* and *Diagram.* Find more work by him at moonbears.biz.